~~that~~

~~one~~

~~time~~

we

were

~~almost~~

people

that one time we were almost people
© Christian Czanlecki / Cathexis Northwest Press

No part of this book may be reproduced without written permission of the publisher or author, except in reviews and articles.

First Printing: 2020

Paperback ISBN: 978-1-7342842-2-5

Cover art by C. M. Tollefson
Designed and edited by C. M. Tollefson

Cathexis Northwest Press

cathexisnorthwestpress.com

that

one

time

we

were

almost

people

by

Christian Czaniecki

Cathexis Northwest Press

Table of Contents

All of the stars, all of them	10
Don't believe the plants when they tell you they have your best interests in mind	11
Something resembling the movement of bodies around another something	13
First it was funny, then it was a fire	16
It's the Clitoris or the end of Childhood	18
Capricious	21
America from a distance	25
Dead Birds of New Zealand	28
A Truncated Genealogy of the Ocean	29
Feed me rocks and seeds and let me alone to die	31
Everything, maybe?	32
Spizella Arborea	33
Don't start telling the truth now	35

All of the stars, all of them

I saw a woman from a distance
in the square off Cuba Street
in her belly she was carrying all
of the world's stars round like the
future or the most perfect expression
of gravity as if any moment she
might lay down and put her feet
on a bench and scream 10,000
birds flying forth from her pussy

I have a sketchbook that lights
itself on fire every time I close it
burning in pastels so bright they
can only exist in complete madness
& making the rubbing plastic noises
of crickets when they are afraid
When I tried to draw her
my pen curled like a snake
& drowned itself in a puddle

I didn't know how to tell her
she was holding everything
I wanted & am terrified of
There is only so much time
for making things that might
unmake themselves later
I've never wanted to love
or hurt something enough
to bring it into the now

Don't believe the plants when they tell you they have your best interests in mind

Did you see there was
          & then there wasn't
a coffin
        shaped like
a   bird
              & full of birds

    Should something

like that be buried
      or burned

                     Probably both
    Smoke
              stops rising
  when no one

is watching it
              Plants
that move towards the sun
     do so in
secret

Lying about where they will be

    One day a bud
the next day a balloon

                         so blue
it's dangerous to be alone with

   No one knows what

happens after you
                   die

take that to mean

                        nothing here
            is worth
coming back for
                                    Smile more

the birds will be

        alive when we
bury them
            dead when they burn

When I was young I was afraid
of everything I got older and realized
I was being overly conservative
Have you ever slept long enough
for your hair to change colors
A tree gone green to red
as a moment so bright that it breaks
every heart in existence
When I was a boy I was terrified
the trees were growing into my room
to carry me away. Every place I'd ever
seen was wonderful until I got there
& it was full of people or worse
I was alone

Something resembling the movement of bodies around another something

I went east or west
                its a fucking globe so
                what the fuck ever

& suddenly I was important
          enough to be missed
                    like a basket

other people
put ideas in
        & set adrift down
                    a stream so   a kindly
                                                    native woman

                    will adopt & raise them
    as their own

until they can come back
to the west
reclaim their rightful place
in the patriarchy
& keep the indigenous
outfits/skills at doing stuff
Hollywood has given me
some issues
with representing the world
when it isn't as white
as well white

I'm sorry
about this next part
when your dream

is actually as empty
inside of me
as it was inside of you

There are more cats
than temples in Thailand
& the sun sets

with the same
laconic pace
as anywhere people live

long enough to think
it is important to watch
Temple cats will follow you around

but they won't
love you forever
the prayers are appropriately

priced and beautiful
You aren't here
& sometimes I am too

both of our dreams are real
at least as long
as the horizon remains

in the distance and the temple
cats loll in the sun
like indolent guardians

or the interspersed bodies
of men who have
learned to pray

honestly

still as pressed wood
buddha's in hawker stalls
gathering the dust

of a million breaths
of a million lung full
of the particulate haze

that makes the sunset
beautiful and slowly
kills the world

First it was funny, then it was a fire

One of the things
I wrote down was
meant to be funny

I can't remember
what it was the words
turned into an animal

it wasn't a wolf & when
it opened its mouth
it exploded into light

& marbles made of
whale bones I mailed
all the pieces I could

back to Chris & asked
him to give them as
gifts in case I never

leave New Zealand I'm
being silly it's going
to be night forever

unless I open my
eyes I wish this bag
wasn't over my head

I can see right through
it but it's messing up
my hair & this is the

season when things
nest in there & so
many things are

dying everywhere
all the time That
building was

a forest the lobby
is painted like a
forest the people

inside sell paper
towels and stationary
I started writing on

the lobby floor in
chalk & the whole
building went up

in flames I don't
know if there was
laughing or screaming

at least part of what
I wrote was funny
the last word was
madness

It's the Clitoris or the end of Childhood

Does anyone really know what happened
to the rest of our childhood

there was youngness   like a tooth
              we were wiggling free
in our mouths
then it fell out
& we
immediately regretted

not having it there

It's like there was endless wonder

fumbling in the dark

with someone else's
buttons and sinking
a hand into tight
denim spaces
blue & grain soft

like a mouth lined
with skin & cotton

interpreting breath and body pressure
like abstract art or an ancient language
      erased by music

This far is good   That far is not

Then POOF
the clitoris

Confetti

Now everything is confined
dollars per square foot
work parties
matching a vase
to your neighbors

expectations

pretending that your hands remember
what to do when faced
with an unfamiliar

body

This is a penis
faster poof
less confetti

If you give dolphins or boys

a mirror they will
stare at their junk.

Did you find the place
where we lose things

can we lose

every shirtless selfie, drunken text, profession of undying & aimless love

Take your shirt off

& poof

you're an asshole

Take this pill to stop your head
from exploding

it will also make you grow

feathers

There are only two solutions
to a broken heart

Both of them are human sacrifice

Your neighbor criticizes your
rose bush(es)
you scream into

a vase and mail it to him

Someone in the office found a clitoris
they weren't supposed to

& poof

everyone is wearing black
robes   carrying knives & torches

I'm not going to anymore parties
with you

I'm staying home to binge watch
dolphin videos
and scream
until it turns to

confetti

Capricious — rooted from the Italian word capriccio which in turn derives from capo "head" and riccio, the word for "hedgehog". Someone who shuddered in fear then was said to have a "hedgehog head"

Given enough time to realize
the inevitable and unenviable
end of their choices even
flowers stop moving towards
the sun   sprout   rise skyward
wilt

I saw a young girl drunk & fallen
into a puddle of her own vomit
ringed by her friends crooning
birds shaped like trumpets
the girls face half lovely & childish
half covered in her insides
I bought her a liter of water
a pile of napkins because
that would have happened
to me alone

I have been piling pieces
of glass and bird feathers
like a totem in the park
by my flat   The sun
hits it in the morning &
everything turns to

bright sky
bright water
like it had
electrified
the most perfectly
blue ever

Almost immediately
after it falls over & the world
is still the world but no one
is alone again

There is no good left
in the world
              but
      not
                      to worry
there isn't really
      any bad
                  either

There is nothing like
a good oversimplification
Apples are essentially a sex
organ. I'll leave that there for
you

One hundred times in a row
the sky makes me feel small
just once it doesn't & I keep looking

You told me once you would love
me forever   one day
that will mean the same thing
to both of us

On the same day I think
everything around us will
turn to stars

Sometimes I'm afraid
                    I'm not
        going to get
what
          I want
Sometimes that I will lose
      what
                  I have

Everything here is mine
not by force or right or need
but the ardent wanting inside

everything that lets gravity
pull stars into the center
of the universe   You
said one thing

      & I swallowed
all existence
I opened
                    my mouth
& the world
      went blind

You know this is just what
you wanted I'm wrapped up
in bed sheets & lost
flailing & drowning in linen
& the fear that only means
the world will end differently
than I want it to

I had just told a train it's velocity
was insignificant.   it wasn't

Outside the rain is more
or less involved in everything
hard at work making all of it
less beautiful   there are 40
geese
        that don't
belong in the middle
    of the road
facing
        each other
    staring into

Their partners tiny geese
eyes

Then they explode from left
to right except the two in the
center that make geese noises

fly off

I walk past all the feathers
spread like confetti
Somebody won this war
most didn't

I'm still
              wrapped
        in sheets
like a child
                      practicing
being a ghost

In a minute the wind will
blow
              I'll either
        explode
or fly off with you

America from a distance

I am going to be friends
with my neighbors cat
until one of us decides
to eat the other

Hunger is a way to want
with a purpose   the simplest
        kind of prayer
                the body says
 to the mind
        & repeats

I just saw the only cloud

that looks like   nothing
then it turned into
madness

How did the day get long
        enough to seem
                like a good
        idea

I had 7 new feathers today
        part of their purpose
                was to be counted

People have been moving
rocks between themselves
& the ocean for millennia

It only took me a week to
learn to

                        fly

In my country people won't

                        give up their guns
but everyone else has to
                        give up porn

Americans look just as stupid
from the sky as they do
in person

I finally flew high enough to see
                        God
            We didn't speak

I haven't learned to land

yet

Children think
            that most adults are full
of shit

That is why people keep shooting them

At some point
            even my heart
      is going to stop
                        beating

I left it in a box
            hooked up to a car battery
the chimpanzee
      guarding it only knows
                        three words
            He is better
                  at praying
      than I will ever be

The ocean keeps moving closer

Americans are
      the only ones
      who know

      why

                & lie about it

Someone put a flower
          next to a dead child
    no one
        had ever seen
        anything
so red

If we lie still long enough
the grass will grow up
around us in castles
nearly tall enough to save
us from the ocean

It's not really my heart in that box

Dead Birds of New Zealand

Take a moment to consider the rose bush
as a colonial construct   Adolescence
as a function of western excess   Gender

There are more bone(s) in your
hand than there are rose(s)
I made that up there are 22
bones in your hand & infinite
roses

Wellington harbor was shaped
by a taniwha or a volcano
depending on who you ask
Then the British Every one
agrees that they did that
I was made by sex
privilege & probably heroin
Definitely

A Truncated Genealogy of the Ocean

All of the world's birds
have gathered to watch
another bird dive into

the white cresting
of a wave like shell
fragments blown in
a circle of wind across

the wet glass of
a perfectly drawn eye

Who put those
balloons here
this was supposed
to be
                                      a funeral

Every dead thing
       is the reintroduction

of carbon
                    nobody needs
                    into
                              the ecosystem

The alternative is living
                    forever
which

                could be

                              worse.

I could point you to
a poem about life
or death but we are

in one & it's about to
be full of the bones
of so many things all
of them blue as a thorn
songs no one remembers
all the bones laid out
in a diagram shaped like
the universe ready to
        explode

In a closed
                      system
            nothing
is ever
        lost

                The most
unfortunate
thing
about living
                      it never

ends

Feed me rocks and seeds and let me alone to die

People have taken   to
throwing rocks   &
birdseed at me   I

I went to the park and buried my arm to the wrist in the wet shadow of the earth
like an ostrich or some distorted plant left over from the Pleioscene

Have been bathing   in
a fountain   the
water sliding off   of
me into oily   rain-
bows flattened   out
smoke as parts   of
the sky wash   out
of my feathers   which
is to say I   prob-
ably deserve   the
stones.

I intended to say for 7 days until I saw god or the curvature of the earth, an hour later
I was eating dumplings on Boulcott Street fumbling chopsticks with my left hand

I haven't wanted   to
fly in weeks   the
sky is so vast   even
god occasionally   loses
itself that explains   a
lot of what happens   when
words mean less   than
ever when they   are
said all at once   the
dogs all howl   in
agony power   goes
out everywhere   for
3 seconds

My right hand held towards the sky, black mud drying brown on my skin
I am a failure

31

Everything, maybe?

I just realized that everything
wait
   what could I possibly know
     about that
      I have only a handful
of bird feathers
        & a scar
the color of the wind
   to show for all the years
of my life.

You learned how to know me the way
I wanted. Afraid &
impressed that I could feel

enough to
circuitously I meant to say I love you
or at least the parts of you that loved
me back, the rest is useless to me.

There was just a moment
   ago
an owl perched on
the chair
across from me
his head turned completely
around &
he exploded into confetti

         the sound
the night makes when
  you need
      ~~aloneness~~ (something?)
& immediately regret
  ~~having it.~~
  (Everything)

Spizella Arborea

America hasn't killed all
of its birds yet but it will

A rejection of science has
lead to the failure of thermo-
dynamics in practice &
sparrows have been falling

at my feet like sputtering mud
stained engines. Charcoal
trying to burn under
water. I've been collecting

them in my bag & carrying
them around like chirping
ghosts feeding them bits
of my hands & my heart.

Whispering forbidden bird
songs to them. All the music
is owned & the sparrows can't
afford to buy back their own

voices from iTunes. I'm
going to take them west
to the desert painted in
the colors of weathered

skin golden a tooth
& scarred by the wind &
persistence of living.
I take the birds one by

one from the bag & press
them against a mesa until
they turn into petroglyphs
so they can disappear the

way they were meant to
worn away by the wind
or boredom.

Don't start telling the truth now

Don't tell me that isn't the sun
just because you're holding my
eyes in your palm like prayer
beads or marbles made of
fury and amber I've

had enough words for forever
they are spilling out of my pockets
I try to feed them to pigeons
stuff them into cards
mail them to
anyone else
leave them laying on
counters like American
pennies worth less
than what it takes to make them
only useful if you're cheap or broke

I can't remember what
I owed
why it made me pluck
my eyes out

I can't see anything but the long
shadow stretching up a sleeve to
the part in everybody that is only funny
for other people I don't see now I
experience

that's code for drowning

I'll tell you about something go
in my coat pocket near my armpit
I'm hiding the funny words there
you can organize them however
you want   just don't touch me

I have a very delicate
flower growing out
of my heart
it's bluer than a wolf
& pretty
this means
I am made entirely
out of glass

Christian was born in Pittsburgh, Pennsylvania. In 2007 he received an MFA from Queens University of Charlotte and promptly quit writing for 10 years. When he returned to writing he brought with him the actual experiences of life he imagined and tried to convey in his earlier poems. He currently lives in Baltimore with his wife Morgan and his cat Fish. He teaches 12th grade English and Special Education and does other things sometimes.

Also Available From Cathexis Northwest Press

<u>God's Love Is Very Busy</u>
by David Seung

<u>Suburban Hermeneutics</u>
by Ian Cappelli

<u>Something To Cry About</u>
by Robert T. Krantz

<u>Fever Dream/Take Heart</u>
by Valyntina Grenier

Cathexis Northwest Press

www.ingramcontent.com/pod-product-compliance
Lightning Source LLC
Chambersburg PA
CBHW021639080526
44584CB00015BA/1596